Original title:
The Multiverse Monologues

Copyright © 2025 Creative Arts Management OÜ
All rights reserved.

Author: Riley Hawthorne
ISBN HARDBACK: 978-1-80567-853-3
ISBN PAPERBACK: 978-1-80567-974-5

Chronicles of the Choices We Wove

In a universe where socks go and flee,
I once wore a green one, my dad wore a spree.
I tripped on a cat that had plans for a shindig,
Then danced with a ghost who just wanted to dig.

Each choice that I made led me here, oh so funny,
To a potluck with aliens who all thought I was honey.
They brought all their dishes, a sight to behold,
I sampled their orange stew, claimed it was bold.

Last Friday I sneezed, and a wormhole appeared,
I zoomed to a planet where no one ever feared.
They giggled in colors, a sight quite bizarre,
While I tried to explain who we are from afar.

But through every twist, I weave tales that delight,
Like fending off dragons with a glowstick at night.
In a realm made of jellybeans, laughter will burst,
Each choice leads me here, oh, where do I thirst?

Intrigues from Points Unknown

In a realm where socks get lost,
Wormholes are simply chaos tossed.
One universe has cats that bake,
While dogs debate their lunchtime break.

Spinning tops dance with glee,
As jellybeans float in cosmic sea.
Here aliens munch on pickle pie,
As toe-socks rhyme and giggle high.

Etchings of Existence's Unsung

Beneath the stars, toaster fights,
For the best of breakfast bites.
One world where all the toast is burnt,
Even the butter feels the burnt!

Chickens in tuxedos strut,
While squirrels in top hats discuss and strut.
In the park, the benches sneeze,
And trees chuckle in the breeze.

Dialogues of the Yet to Come

Future phones will talk in rhyme,
While calendars slow their time.
In one spot, the fish can sing,
And in another, cats take wing.

Toasters chat about the toast,
While dancing forks claim they're the most.
A world where beards grow on cars,
And coffee comes from chocolate jars.

Portraits in Parallel

In a place where penguins wear shades,
And cows cheat at poker parades.
Where hats can giggle, shoes can dance,
And time machines just hate a glance.

Here rainbows taste like cotton candy,
While earthworms find it all quite dandy.
A universe where laughter's prime,
And joy is measured out in time.

Portraits of What Might Have Been

In a world where cats can talk,
They argue over who's the boss.
Socks are treasure, milk's a rock,
Fish fly by, and all's a gloss.

Maybe I'm a knight with flair,
Fighting goblins made of cheese.
With a sword that's just a chair,
I rule the land with playful ease.

In another life, I'm a bird,
Singing songs of ancient lore.
Through clouds of fluff, I've surely stirred,
My feathers bright, I dance and soar.

Oh, if I'd learned to play the lute,
Perhaps I'd charm the moon tonight.
Instead, I sit here, none so astute,
With peanut butter, on toast, I bite.

Echoing Contemplations of Existence

If I were cheese upon a plate,
Would mice bring gifts to dance around?
Or would they only contemplate,
How to nibble without a sound?

In a world where goldfish run,
Would it be strange to wear their hats?
Do they complain, "This isn't fun!"
While we quibble about our mats?

Perhaps I'm really a bold chair,
Surveying all that's lost in time.
Folk sit with secrets, bites to share,
While I just wait for a punchline rhyme.

In another life, I'm a shoe,
Stomping through puddles, kicking spry.
With laughter echoing, skies so blue,
I'd dream of adventures as I fly.

Chronicles of Eternal Possibilities

One day, I'll be a talking frog,
Wearing glasses made from twigs.
Guess I'll croak and join the fog,
As they whistle songs and do jigs.

In a realm where spoons are wise,
They'll debate soup of the day.
"Chunky or smooth?"—the great reprise,
While forks just roll their eyes and sway.

What if I'm a pop-up book,
Living pages bright and grand?
With each turn, a new hook,
Where dragons play in far-off lands.

Another me, a disco ball,
Reflecting laughter from the floor.
Spinning tales at every call,
While glitter sticks like friendship's score.

Flickers of Existence Across Time

I once was dust upon a shelf,
Contemplating life's great hues.
Or maybe I was just myself,
Mixed in these eccentric shoes.

In that other life, I snack,
On clouds of cotton candy dreams.
Sipping lemonade, cut no slack,
Life's full of whimsical schemes.

What if I were a lightbulb's glow,
Brightening minds unknown to space?
I'd flicker thoughts that come and go,
While shadows dance, and dreams embrace.

A moment flashes: I'm a cat,
Juggling fish in silly ways.
Keeping score, "Look at that!"
I'd purr through mischief all my days.

Threads of Unseen Realities

In worlds where cats can talk,
And dogs are taking walks,
People juggling flying pies,
And giggling at the skies.

A universe made of cheese,
With mice in tailored fleece,
Dancing on a rainbow's end,
Just waiting for the next trend.

With hats upon their heads so grand,
They dance across a cotton land,
While bearded clams recite a rhyme,
Making fun of passing time.

Each place a peculiar game,
Where nothing is quite the same,
With comets who wear glitter shoes,
And tell the best dad jokes for views.

Tapestry of Diverging Lives

In one, a fish rides a bike,
While squirrels opt for a hike,
Everyone wears socks on hands,
Building castles made of cans.

A realm where toast takes a leap,
And veggies laugh as they sleep,
With pudding pots on every shelf,
Singing songs to please themselves.

There's a spider that plays the flute,
And a frog in a four-piece suit,
Each laugh echoes down the lane,
As giggles dance like summer rain.

Oh, what a world of silly sights,
With kite-flying squirrels in tights,
Realities woven with flair and glee,
In this land of the bizarre and free.

Reflections in Cosmic Mirrors

In mirrors where ducks wear crowns,
And witches fly upside down,
Balloon animals have debates,
On matters of jelly and states.

Things spin in a merry-go-round,
Where laughter's the only sound,
And pizza pies hold a ball,
Inviting friends both big and small.

Here, in this mirror's play,
Cats will challenge dogs to sway,
While clouds tickle our silly heads,
With giggles filling up our beds.

Each glance shows a wacky scene,
Where unicorns wear jeans of green,
In these mirrors of cosmic grace,
We find joy in every face.

Chronicles of Alternate Paths

Once upon a time in style,
A robot danced a funky mile,
Telling tales of flying spoons,
And singing songs to comical tunes.

Across the street, a wallaby,
Danced with glee, so wild and free,
Wearing hats made out of pies,
And cracking jokes about the skies.

Each step leads to silly fate,
Pickles debating on a plate,
As time-traveling bears discuss,
Who made the best peanut butter with us.

In these tales of strange delight,
Where laughter shines so very bright,
A world of chaos and pure cheer,
Is where we truly hold dear.

Parables of Forgotten Echoes

In a realm where socks go to hide,
A hundred pair, each with pride.
They argue over missing mates,
While dust bunnies keep their gates.

The wise old chair, it shakes and creaks,
Chasing dreams that no one seeks.
It tells of worlds where cats are kings,
And every sparrow's voice still sings.

Here toast lands buttered side down,
And squirrels wear crowns in each town.
The sun sleeps late and wakes with glee,
In this land of pure folly, that's key.

They dance on clouds and slide on air,
While ice cream flows without a care.
With laughter echoing left and right,
These parables bring absurd delight.

Scribbles on Time's Canvas

A clock with hands that twist and turn,
Counts all the minutes we never learn.
The past insists it knows the score,
While future whispers, 'What's in store?'

Pencil-thin figures scribble dreams,
In colors that burst at the seams.
They paint the world in polka dots,
As logic melts in sugar plots.

Each tick a giggle, each tock a cheer,
Time filed a complaint, said, 'It's not fair!'
While crayons march in lines so bold,
Telling tales of chaos untold.

Waves of whimsy wash over the floor,
As imagination opens its door.
In laughter, a canvas forms anew,
Where scribbles dance in a vibrant hue.

Paths Laced with Alternative Histories

In a world where toast is always brown,
And monkeys wear the royal gown.
Napoleon lost to a turtle race,
While history laughs, just in case.

Here, every pirate's lost their hook,
Now they barter with a cookbook.
And kings sit down to tea with mice,
Trading secrets that come with spice.

A wizard forgot his own spell's end,
Now every cat is just a friend.
The chairs have banded, formed a crew,
To fight the dust, as heroes do.

Paths twist and twine under the moon,
Where everyone dances to their tune.
In laughter and folly, stories collide,
With joy that ignites like a thrilling ride.

Constellations of Choice and Destiny

Stars debate who shines the best,
While planets play a game of chess.
A comet swoops with ice cream tails,
And laughter echoes in rosy trails.

Each choice a star, a blink, a spark,
Illuminating paths through the dark.
Constellations bend to make it right,
While light years sing through the magic night.

Timelines tumble through cosmic dust,
A leap of faith, a hitch in trust.
The universe giggles at our plight,
As we tumble down choices in flight.

With every twist, the stardust gleam,
Turns choices into a wild dream.
A whimsical dance of fate and chance,
In this grand and hilarious cosmic dance.

Letters from Alternate Lives

I wrote a letter to myself,
From a world where I'm a shelf.
I sit each day, collecting dust,
While my mates all laugh and gust.

In another tome, I'm quite a cat,
Purring as I chase my hat.
Eating fish and napping proud,
No worries, just a sunny cloud.

Then there's me as a cup of tea,
Sipping sweetly, blissfully free.
But when the coffee came around,
Oh dear, I barely made a sound.

A letter from my hyper self,
Riding on a wild shelf.
With letters from me all around,
Their chaos makes the world astound.

Dreams in Multiple Dimensions

I dreamt last night I was a chair,
Being sat upon without a care.
Though nacho cheese spilled on my back,
It made for quite the comfy crack.

In another realm, a fish on land,
I flopped around, it felt so grand.
Waving fins to all the gents,
A swim meet held in my defense.

Oh, the time I was a silly sock,
Trapped in shoes; it was a shock!
I played it cool, despite the haze,
Dancing feet in wild ballet.

A dragon once, with wings so wide,
But forgot my flight, what a ride!
I tumbled down, landed in a pie,
The best dessert, oh my oh my!

Fragments of Forgotten Realities

In a world where cats rule the day,
I serve my feline, in disarray.
With tiny crowns and royal naps,
While I clean up their silly mishaps.

I once was toast, burned on one side,
In a breakfast brawl, I had to bide.
The butter wars are thrilling, you see,
Fighting off jam, just let me be!

Then I shot some hoops as a green bean,
Dribbling down with a mighty sheen.
But the basket was high, beyond my reach,
Guess I'm destined for veggie speech!

A book that spoke, oh what a sight,
With pages fluttering, oh so bright.
But all it said was "Read me twice!"
Oh, the books do have their vice!

Songs of Celestial Convergence

In the sky, I danced with stars,
Singing tunes on my guitar.
But space was loud with echoes bright,
I tripped on Mars and lost my flight.

On Saturn's rings, we formed a band,
Playing tunes with a cosmic hand.
But the aliens just did a jig,
While I forgot the lyrics, oh so big!

Singing high like a comet's tail,
A melody that told a tale.
But gravity pulled me back with force,
Now I'm grounding, feeling hoarse.

With supernovae blocking my beats,
We jammed out tunes with cosmic feats.
A galactic concert, loud and grand,
But my mic was just a piece of sand!

Revelations from Beyond the Horizon

In worlds where cats are kings, they say,
Fish ride bikes in a grand relay.
Rain comes down as chocolate sprinkles,
And laughter blooms where time simply crinkles.

Today I met my doppelgänger's cat,
It wore a hat and had a pet bat.
Together we planned a cosmic prank,
To steal a star and paint it pink.

With each new spin we miss the ground,
Gravity's lost, the jokes abound.
Dancing noodles in space parade,
While gummy bears cheer from the lemonade.

So here we twirl, under cosmic lights,
Chasing dreams in peculiar flights.
With every laugh, a new tale spins,
In these worlds, every loss is a win!

Secrets of the Celestial Fabric

Beyond the seams where worlds combine,
I found a sock that smelled of lime.
It danced and twirled, a funky sight,
Claiming it ruled the galaxy's light.

I met a chef who baked with glee,
Cakes that giggled, wild and free.
A slice of pie sang opera loud,
While broccoli formed a cheering crowd.

In one realm, penguins wear cool shades,
Riding scooters through velvet glades.
They laughed at how the world's askew,
Wishing on stars of neon blue.

Each thread we pull reveals a jest,
A universe where humor's best.
So stitch me a tale with laughter spun,
In every blink, a new realm begun!

Harmonies of Forgotten Itineraries

On maps of laughter, we set our course,
Through valleys of whimsy, on a whim, of course.
A hedgehog conductor leads the parade,
With capes of glitter that never fade.

Ticklish mountains try to sneeze,
While rivers giggle as they tease.
We skip along with glee and jest,
In a land where silliness is the best!

All flights delayed by sandwiches grand,
They plot world travel with a peanut butter band.
We hop on chairs that float up high,
To catch the cloud-cakes that bake in the sky.

With every note, a charm unfolds,
Where whimsy whispers and the cosmos scolds.
So let's map our laughs with every stroke,
Surprise awaits in every joke!

Tapestries of Time Untold

In woven threads of dreams untold,
Wormholes where the socks get bold.
Knitting planets with a twisty hand,
Where spaghetti monsters roam this land.

Chronicles of hiccups ripple through space,
As jellybeans jump in a lively race.
Each tick of the clock is a giggly prank,
Surprise confetti from the time bank.

Through lands bizarre, we frolic and sway,
Time travelers lost in a game of play.
A tickle from fate, a wink from chance,
And off we go in a cosmic dance.

So weave me a tale that tickles the mind,
With laughter and joy, so sweetly entwined.
In this web of whimsy where we belong,
Let's sing together our timeless song!

Prophecies of Cosmic Chance

In a universe quite absurd,
Giraffes wear hats, how strangely heard.
Planets dance in a haphazard way,
Cats debate if they should stay.

Squirrels plot to conquer the moon,
While dishes sing a merry tune.
Stars winking in a cosmic jest,
Prophesying who'll be the best.

Fish in spacesuits float by me,
Eating pizza made of brie.
Turtles racing in slow, strange glee,
A world where nothing's as it seems.

Coffee beans that laugh at the grind,
Leaving all earthly worries behind.
In this realm of chance and cheer,
Funny tales are all we hear.

Verses from Shifting Echoes

Echoes travel through time and space,
Chasing shadows at a leisurely pace.
Llamas knitting on the edge of night,
Whimsical dreams take off in flight.

Jellybeans rain from a purple sky,
While old socks debate and sigh.
Grab a seat; join the parade,
Balloons of laughter serenade.

Robots dance in synchronized shoes,
Riding unicorns while sharing news.
Gravitational whims make them twirl,
In a world where nonsense unfurls.

Every moment's a quirky delight,
In shifting echoes, nothing feels right.
Lose yourself in this playful jest,
Where each absurdity's a quest.

Tales Woven by Cosmic Winds

Cosmic winds spin stories anew,
Of dancing marshmallows in blue.
Pirates sail on gummy dreadnoughts,
Squirrels are plotting and tying knots.

Wizards bake cakes made of stars,
While robots drive tiny old cars.
Frogs in tuxedos sing on a stage,
Time travelers turn a new page.

Whimsical creatures weave tales so fine,
Of broccoli forests and sparkling wine.
Laughing at physics, they misbehave,
Making mischief in the cosmic wave.

Each tale's a tickle, a silly thrill,
Fueling our laughter, a timeless spill.
So join in the fun, don't be shy,
Woven tales take us high and high.

Chimeras of the Imagination

In chimera lands where dreams collide,
Hot air balloons on a jellyfish ride.
Over mountains of cotton candy fluff,
Everything here is delightfully tough.

Cactus who tell the best of jokes,
Invite the wise and foolish folks.
Elephants tap dance in a line,
Creating chaos, but it's just fine.

Mirrors reflecting remarkably odd,
A talking fish, a time-traveling god.
With each twist, our hopes take flight,
In this realm, the strange feels just right.

Comedy reigns in imagination's space,
Where dreams giggle in a happy race.
Embrace the fun, the wild, the bright,
Chimeras dance in the moonlit night.

Beyond the Horizons of Now

In one world, cows can sing,
While chickens dance in a ring.
The grass is blue, the sky is green,
Oh, what a sight that must have been!

In another, spoons have wings,
And dream of flying, oh the things!
A fork is king, a knife's a jester,
Dining is a wild, grand fest-er!

In yet another, clocks tick backward,
And all our dreams come much afterward.
We laugh at time, it's quite absurd,
In a world where chaos is preferred!

So let us leap through every door,
With silly giggles and tales galore.
Beyond what we know, there's much to explore,
In lands where laughter is never a bore!

Harmonies from Alternate Echoes

In one realm, cats conduct the band,
While dogs just sit and applaud, so grand.
Fish play drums, and frogs croon low,
What a concert, to and fro!

In a space where rain falls up,
And everyone sips from a teacup.
Spoons play duets with forks in tune,
As the stars wink down at the moon.

In a vibe where laughter's the law,
And everyone dances, sans flaw.
Improv games with a twist so neat,
Where joy and silliness never meet.

So come and join the wild parade,
Where giggles shimmer and pranks cascade.
With harmonies echoed in glee,
We'll sing through realms, just you and me!

Distant Chords of Reality

In a land where waffles wear hats,
And pancake trees host feasting chats.
Bacon sings with a crispy tone,
In this realm, we're never alone!

In another verse, fish ride bicycles,
Hopscotch with frogs in their spectacles.
They laugh and shout 'till the sun comes up,
In a world where joy fills every cup!

In the dimension where socks converse,
Sharing secrets both funny and terse.
They dance in pairs, never alone,
In the soft, cozy place they call home.

Travel with me to this oddity,
Where giggles float in our holiday.
With distant chords that make us sway,
In these silly realms, we'll always play!

Odes to Unseen Horizons

In realms where bridges are made of cheese,
And clouds are soft as a gentle breeze.
The goats wear crowns, the sheep take flights,
In this place of zany delights!

In another scene, shadows are bold,
They tell tales of laughter, never old.
Where socks have pairs, they spin and twirl,
In a twist of fate, they dance and swirl.

In lands where rainbows twirl and twist,
Where giggles bubble like mist.
Each note a splash, every laugh a ray,
In unseen horizons, we'll always stay!

So hop on this ride, let's create some cheer,
Through silly dimensions, we'll wander here.
With odes to the funny and tales of the wild,
We spread our laughter, both adult and child!

Threads of Existence Unraveled

In one world, cats run cars,
And dogs debate in bars.
A penguin flies a plane,
While fish complain of rain.

A toaster sings at night,
As socks escape in flight.
We chase the fridge around,
And find lost socks abound.

In every twist and turn,
The candle starts to burn.
With jellybeans that dance,
And chairs that mock your stance.

If you think it's all strange,
Just wait for the next change.
In every thought we find,
The giggles of the mind.

Mythos of the Infinite Cosmos

In space, the cheese is real,
And moons are made of meal.
The stars play hide-and-seek,
While aliens love to peek.

With planets dressed in styles,
They strut down cosmic aisles.
Galaxies spin and laugh,
And time takes selfies, half.

A comet holds its breath,
While meteors dare to bet.
In a tea shop on Mars,
They sip on Milky Bars.

Yet with every quirk and turn,
The universe will learn.
That laughter is the way,
To brighten up the day.

Traces of Existence Across States

In a land where time loops back,
And nothing stays on track.
The trees tell silly jokes,
And waterfalls are blokes.

With rain that tastes like pie,
And bees that wear a tie,
The hats that wander free,
Are just as nice as me.

Dimensions twist and shout,
While shadows figure out,
How to dance on the street,
With rhythm in their feet.

The bunnies bounce and prance,
While moments take a chance.
In every glance we share,
There's giggles in the air.

Visions from the Quantum Abyss

In a realm where quirks collide,
And logic's tossed aside.
The clocks all melt away,
As colors start to sway.

A ghost plays hide-and-seek,
When cats begin to squeak.
The walls are made of dreams,
Where nothing's ever as it seems.

Dimensions do the twist,
As logic gets dismissed.
With laughter echoing wide,
The universe as our guide.

So come and take a peek,
At truths that feel unique.
In every thought we hold,
There's humor to unfold.

Starlit Dialogues

In a café where stars collide,
A penguin sips some cosmic pride.
He orders ice with a dash of light,
And giggles at a worm in flight.

A cat with wings joins the fray,
She meows in a most peculiar way.
Together they plot a heist so grand,
To steal the moon and make it bland.

An octopus spins tales in the air,
While juggling comets without a care.
The black hole chef prepares a feast,
For creatures strange, to say the least.

As laughter echoes through the skies,
They toast to madness, in sweet surprise.
Reality bends, a whimsical rhyme,
In this café of space and time.

Crossroads of Existence

At the corner of here and there,
A squirrel debates, "Do I dare?"
With a nutty grin and a zany spark,
He hops to dance with a neon shark.

A time traveler coding a song,
Asks, "Is this where I belong?"
Awaiting the bus, he taps his feet,
While googling trends from 2200's street.

A dapper frog wears a top hat bold,
Reciting tales of adventures old.
Yet every glance can show mischief,
As paths collide, like wind and riff.

At this junction, life's a jest,
With options swirling, no time to rest.
They giggle as they wander about,
In a land where there's never a doubt.

Unwritten Tales of Parallel Worlds

In a world where socks are pets,
And shoes compete in dance-offs, bets.
The paperclips hold cosmic chats,
While rulers measure catlike spats.

A door that leads to nowhere fast,
Hides bedtime stories from the past.
Where spoons are kings and forks are knights,
And tea has powers of subtle delights.

A wizard wears a cape of cheese,
While camels discuss the art of breeze.
Each tale unfurls like a zany kite,
In skies adorned with pure delight.

Invisible ink writes laughter loud,
As fables form a vibrant crowd.
In unwritten scripts, they find their way,
A universe of fun every day.

Luminous Shadows of Possibility

In a garden where shadows play,
Glowworms giggle the night away.
A garden gnome sings off-key,
While wishing on a cup of tea.

A butterfly with a pirate hat,
Steals whispers from a sleeping cat.
Together they sketch improbable dreams,
With candy canes and whipped cream streams.

A robot ponders life's big quiz,
While dancing to an ancient fizz.
His circuits buzz with questions bold,
Like 'Can nuts ever be sold cold?'

As shadows stretch and laughter blooms,
They paint the air with goofy tunes.
In each soft glow, a giggle's cast,
In this land where fun will last.

Parallel Whispers

In a universe where socks are lost,
The dryers hold them, at what cost?
Each sock a champion of its plight,
   Debating freedom every night.

On Tuesday, shades of purple dance,
While cats in top hats take a chance.
They juggle yarn and sip on tea,
   Oh, how silly life can be!

One universe sings a tune so sweet,
While another's breakfast is just a beet.
Time-traveling toasts toast their bread,
While in other realms, it's cheese instead.

   Laughing at the cosmic clock,
Where time ticks backwards, what a shock!
In every whisper, a giggle hides,
As we journey on these parallel rides.

Echoes from Infinity

In a realm where penguins fly,
They quack their dreams up in the sky.
Waltzing on clouds with a twinkling eye,
Who knew that fish could really fly?

Echoes bounce with laughter bright,
From worlds where night is always light.
Cereal rains and chocolate streams,
Reality here is not what it seems.

They say in one, the chairs can sing,
And every door has a doorbell ring.
While in another, clouds wear hats,
And squirrels learn to talk with chats.

Listen closely, the whispers tell,
Of worlds where everything's a spell.
Infinite giggles swirl around,
In these echoes where joy is found.

Fragments of Other Dreams

In cities made of melting cheese,
The mice hold parties with utmost ease.
Breadstick towers touch the sky,
As dancing salads flutter by.

With jellybeans as currency,
They bounce around, so carefree.
And in the park, the trees do sway,
Telling jokes in a leafy way.

One realm has cupcakes that can bake,
While others ride on waves of lake.
The gravity pulls in funny ways,
As giggling creatures dance and play.

Fragments of dreams from near and far,
Shimmering bright like a shooting star.
Together they twirl, laugh, and scheme,
In every corner of this dream.

Voices Across Dimensions

Voices travel on cosmic winds,
Where live cats are played by violinists.
They serenade the absent moon,
Whose laughter echoes, an odd tune.

In a world of marshmallow trees,
The squirrels debate how to freeze the breeze.
While rabbits in slippers hop with grace,
Every hop a dance, a joyful race.

Across dimensions, the pranks unfold,
With silly gnomes and stories bold.
Time is a jester, playing tricks,
As laughter rolls like cosmic clicks.

Whispers merge in an endless play,
Where every moment's a chance to sway.
In the playground of realms, we'll spin and twirl,
Creating hilarity in this bizarre whirl.

Unfolding Dreams of Elsewhere

In a world where cows play chess,
And unicorns wear fancy dress,
Turtles race in high-speed chases,
And tea is served in crystal cases.

Flying kangaroos sip tea,
Laughing at the absurdity,
Where every door leads to surprise,
And socks can talk, oh, how they rise!

Worms play guitar, frogs do ballet,
Bananas throw a party each day,
With jellybeans as guests of honor,
These dreams get weirder, a true show-stopper!

So grab your hat, and take a leap,
Into a place where giggles creep,
For each step forward takes you far,
In a land where weird is the superstar!

Constellations of Choice

Stars decide what we should eat,
Pizza or a moldy beet,
The rabbit winks, the owl hoots loud,
As choices swirl in a cosmic crowd.

Should I wear shoes or go barefoot?
What if I eat a cream-filled fruit?
Planets giggle at our flops,
While jellyfish do moonwalks and hops.

Time tickles us with silly pranks,
As we dodge intergalactic tanks,
With every choice a wild surprise,
Spaghetti rains from purple skies!

So here's to choices, let them reign,
In trampoline lands of joy and pain,
May our decisions keep us grinning,
In this cosmic game, let's keep winning!

Shadows in the Web of Fate

Spiders spin tales of daring deeds,
While ants plot heists and plant their seeds,
Each shadow dances with delight,
As fate giggles under the moonlight.

A cat wears glasses, reads the news,
Chasing after dreams, with purple shoes,
The clocks melt into cream-filled pies,
As fate chuckles with mischievous sighs.

When fortune smiles, we take a chance,
To join in on the critter dance,
With tigers tap-dancing on the wall,
Life's a circus—let's have a ball!

So tread softly in fate's soft embrace,
With every twist, find a new space,
For shadows may tickle, tease, and play,
And bring laughter into each strange day!

Conversations Beyond the Veil

Ghosts debate over pizza toppings,
As poltergeists laugh, never stopping,
In the night, they host a show,
With jokes and puns that steal the glow.

Witches brew with a splash of sass,
Summoning laughter from the glass,
While goblins share their favorite memes,
In the realm of mystical dreams.

Mermaids write, sharing ancient lore,
On scrolls made from a dragon's snore,
Each tale filled with giggles and cheer,
For what's a veil without a fun sneer?

So let's join in these charming chats,
Where everyone wears funny hats,
Beyond the veil, life's a delight,
A cozy haunt every starry night!

Tales of Alternate Existence

In one world, cats run the show,
While dogs just sit and watch the glow.
Pigs in capes zoom through the air,
Claiming victory without a care.

In another realm, socks speak a tune,
While rocks wear hats, making big brune.
Toast debates with butter on high,
As pancakes argue, 'We can fly!'

A cow invents a dance routine,
While llamas practice being keen.
Here, fish drive cars, a puzzling sight,
And ants hold concerts every night.

The doors of fate swing wide and bright,
To worlds where wrong seems just so right.
In laughter's grasp, we twist and bend,
As antics spark, and giggles blend.

Harmonies of Diverging Paths

One path leads to a land of spry,
Where vegetables can laugh and cry.
Talking carrots, witty and spry,
Claiming, 'We're not just here to fry!'

Another road, with shoes that leap,
Where dreams can swim and wishes creep.
The skies pour candy instead of rain,
And vacation's budget is quite insane.

In a quirky nook, the sun yodels high,
While chairs debate if they can fly.
Tacos waltz on taco Tuesday,
And everyone looks forward to play.

With each twist and turn, the laughter swells,
As harmony is found in jest and spells.
In paths diverging, joy's the aim,
And every crisis turns to fame.

Conversations with Shadows of Fate

Shadows whisper secrets, quite absurd,
In corners where the quirky birds.
'Why so serious?' grins a chair,
As shadows join with utmost flair.

A shadow pranks the sun above,
Saying, 'Why not shine with a hug of love?'
While moonbeams giggle, tickle their wit,
And stars join dance, eager to fit.

Fate's a joker with cards up his sleeve,
Daring the cosmos to believe.
Juggling planets with a cheesy grin,
In this realm, everyone wins!

Come join the chat, the lights may flicker,
As timeless tales emerge, they snicker.
In every shadow, a story awaits,
With laughter echoing through the gates.

Journeys Through the Cosmic Tapestry

On a comet's tail, a squirrel rides,
Through space's wonders and playful tides.
The stars all giggle, keeping the score,
While cosmic jellybeans dance on the floor.

Planets spin gossip about their moons,
While meteors hum their funny tunes.
Ancient comets catch ride to the past,
In laughter's embrace, they're free at last.

Time travelers swap old dad jokes,
Over tea brewed by wise old folks.
Through this grand tapestry, we intertwine,
In bursts of joy, our souls align.

Each stitch a moment, woven and bright,
Lighting the dark with joy, not fright.
Exploring the cosmos, we find our way,
Through laughter, peace reigns every day.

Interstellar Musings

In a realm where cats wear hats,
And turtles dance on beams of light,
I sip my tea with little bats,
While constellations giggle at night.

A planet made of candy dreams,
Where aliens play hopscotch with stars,
They munch on asteroids with gleams,
And race on comets, leaving scars.

Jellybeans rain from crimson skies,
While moonbeams tickle bunnies' toes,
And wise old owls share grand old lies,
As drowsy robots sip their prose.

In black holes that sing jazzy tunes,
And wormholes wrapping 'round their friends,
I find the humor in these goons,
And ponder where this madness ends.

Variations on a Celestial Theme

Once I met a star named Fred,
Who wore bright shoes and chains of gold,
He claimed that planets danced instead,
And whispered secrets yet untold.

Comets with their funky styles,
Skated through the cosmic breeze,
While asteroids exchanged their smiles,
In lightyears spent with such great ease.

Venus baked a pie so sweet,
It floated gently through the air,
Sirens sang with voices neat,
As chocolate rain began to share.

Meanwhile, Martians played charades,
With Earthlings caught up in the plot,
Unraveling their wacky trades,
In timeless fun, they forgot.

Disparate Echoes of Utopia

In a world where socks are paired,
And penguins fly through raging seas,
Life's absurd, but none are scared,
While monkeys teach philosophy.

Planets play a game of chess,
With galaxies forming their teams,
Each move, a gleeful, wild mess,
Wagered on their candy dreams.

How ridiculous the news can be,
As robots argue left or right,
While spaghetti worms twirl with glee,
In this cosmic comic delight.

Stars hold up their glowing signs,
Inviting others to their party,
In quirky rhythms, all align,
Life's a dance, so wild and hearty.

Mosaic of Infinite Journeys

I took a trip through time and space,
Where chickens wore tuxedos grand,
They strutted by with utmost grace,
And danced upon a cosmic strand.

A dolphin drove a shiny car,
With wannabe astronauts in tow,
They laughed about just being bizarre,
While shooting stars put on a show.

Hitchhiking on a rainbow's end,
I stumbled on a jelly fish,
Who offered secrets, loves to send,
And granted every wacky wish.

Adventures folded like a map,
Into a pocket stitched with dreams,
And as I napped, I heard a clap,
From parallel worlds and their schemes.

Riddles of Reality's Weave

In a world where cats can fly,
Dogs wear hats and learn to sigh,
Coffee brews with a wink and grin,
Pigeons dance like they're at a spin.

Toast that sings, and jam that jives,
Socks that giggle, and bread that thrives,
Reality bends, twists, and larks,
In this place, even shadows spark!

Bouncing thoughts on trampoline skies,
Where dreams can juggle and laughter flies,
A universe looped with cosmic cheer,
Join the parade, hop on, my dear!

So chase those riddles, light and sound,
In this quirky realm, where joy is found,
Let's weave a tapestry, bright and bold,
In the fabric of fun, watch tales unfold!

Melodies from the Edge of Infinity

From beyond the stars, a tune takes flight,
Singing fish wearing hats at night,
Swinging moons with jazzy beats,
Dancing comets on candy streets.

Ticklish clouds and wobbly suns,
Tick-tock laughter, all in puns,
A symphony spun on a giant plate,
Where time and space politely wait.

Marshmallow clouds hum soft refrains,
While unicorns juggle in rainbow chains,
Each note a dash of cosmic whim,
In this wacky world, let's dance on a limb!

So grab your hats and twirl around,
Join the music where joy is found,
At the edge of infinity, you will see,
Life's a melody, come play with me!

Echoing Thoughts of the Universe

Echoes bounce in the cosmic halls,
Where gravity trips and giggles fall,
Thoughts like balloons float up so high,
In a universe painted with pie in the sky.

Silly quarks that wear bow ties,
Lizards recite Shakespeare, oh my,
While bees buzz poetry on honey toast,
In this realm, weird is the most!

Invisible friends hold tea parties grand,
On a comet's tail, making their stand,
Witty whispers from stars above,
Crafting laughter with every shove.

So ponder away, let ideas stray,
In this echo chamber where giggles play,
Thoughts looping 'round like a rollercoaster,
Join the fun, be a cosmic boaster!

The Language of Divergent Thoughts

Words that dance on the tip of a pen,
Fizzing like soda, time and again,
Conversations with trees, so wise and frank,
Playful banter, in colors they prank!

A snail's opinion on shoes quite neat,
While frogs debate on who's got the beat,
Chickens chat about existential plights,
In a world where nonsense takes flight!

Languages sprout like flowers in May,
With ticks and tocks that playfully sway,
Silly syllables tickle the air,
Crafting stories that sparkle and share.

So let's embrace these quirky sounds,
Where laughter and joy are always found,
In this grand tapestry of thought's delight,
Divergent ideas gleam in the light!

The Symphony of Possible Lives

In one world, I'm a cat, lounging all day,
Chasing sunbeams, dreaming away.
In another, a chef, my soufflés take flight,
A sprinkle of chaos, my kitchen's delight.

Maybe I'm a hero, cape flapping with flair,
Saving the day while I fix my hair.
Or a potato, just sit and relax,
Living the dream with no pressure, no tax!

A world where I dance like a penguin on ice,
Flapping my wings, oh, isn't that nice?
Or a unicorn prancing, all sparkles and glee,
Teaching the world what it means to be free.

So many lives, oh so much to explore,
I'll try them all—who could ask for more?
For every choice leads to a brand new scene,
Life's a comedy, oh how we've been keen!

Reflections of What Could Be.

In one universe, I'm a trendy chair,
Sitting in style, without a care.
Another, a fish, with bubbles to blow,
Swimming in circles, just putting on a show.

Perhaps a ghost, I haunt my own house,
Scaring my future self, like a silly spouse.
Or a talking shoe, giving fashion advice,
"Wear more pink," I'd shout, "that'll be nice!"

There's a world where I'm a bold lemon tree,
Sour but zesty, oh can you see?
A broccoli superhero, saving the day,
Flashing my florets, in a veggie ballet!

In every blink, choices twist and turn,
Endless laughter in each lesson we learn.
I'll raise a toast to the lives I might lead,
A quirky buffet—a smorgasbord indeed!

Echoes of Infinite Realms

Picture me a cloud, floating so high,
Tickling the birds as they swoosh by.
Or a sock lost in the laundry's embrace,
Adventuring on roads, oh what a chase!

Perhaps I'm a jam, set in a jar,
Spreading some joy, not traveling far.
Or the last slice of pizza, oh what a dream,
Always in-demand, the star of the theme!

A couch potato in a race with a snail,
"Catch me if you can!" I'd gleefully wail.
In another, I'm a pencil, scribbling fate,
Writing wild stories, all while I wait.

With echoes resounding across the vast space,
Each quirk a delight, each twist a new face.
So let's laugh out loud, no worry or fear,
In this comedic realm, all lives we endear!

Whispers from Parallel Dimensions

In one lane, I'm a snail, oh so swift,
Breaking land speed records—what a gift!
In another, a broomstick, sweeping the skies,
Bristling with joy, oh how time flies!

Maybe a monkey, in a swing of delight,
Cracking some jokes with a banana in sight.
Or a jester, hopping with foolish grace,
Poking fun at kings, oh what a place!

Consider me a light bulb, brightening dreams,
Flickering laughter, bursting at seams.
Or a cheeky raccoon, dumpster-diving at night,
Finding lost treasures, a true pale moonlight!

Each dimension's whisper leads to a grin,
Life's bizarre choices, oh where to begin?
So let's parade through these whims so profound,
In a whimsical world, endless joy's found!

Philosophies from Shattered Horizons

In a world where socks go missing,
I ponder if they're just out kissing.
Dimension doors swing wide and loud,
Chasing dreams in a wink, it's allowed.

Cats with jobs and dogs that read,
Plants that argue on how to succeed.
Each step takes a twist, a loop, a twirl,
In this fleeting, silly, quirky whirl.

Gravity laughs, it pulls me in,
As I chase my thoughts on a feathered pin.
Life's a circus with a painted throne,
Somewhere a clone is brewing scone.

So I tip my hat to the cosmic jest,
In this race of oddities, I do my best.
With every surprise, I grin and wiggle,
For in strange worlds, I dance and giggle.

Musing on Unexplored Pathways

A squirrel in a tux on Tuesday night,
Dances with glee in the weird moonlight.
Rabbits read novels and toast with tea,
Where's the cat that just fled with my key?

Parallel timelines, a game of spin,
My doppelgänger's winning with a mischievous grin.
Should I join him in a prank or two?
Or just binge on snacks like I always do?

Through unseen doors, I gather peeks,
At universes filled with raccoon shrieks.
From bizarre to absurd, I take my shot,
In this patchwork quilt, I've hit the jackpot.

The road less taken plays in reverse,
Each twist and turn, the universe's verse.
So let's laugh together, all roads will blend,
On this cosmic journey, fun has no end.

Contemplations of Echoing Enigmas

A rubber duck floats in the stars,
Debating physics with cookie jars.
Time travelers come just to eat,
As the universe dances on tiny feet.

Whispers of ghosts wearing sun hats,
Pondering life over chats with cats.
Grumpy time lords sipping hot stew,
In this space-time riddle, who's who?

The universe giggles at its own mess,
Creating wonders we can't quite guess.
With each silly notion, I scribble my fits,
Cackling at quirks as reality splits.

In echoing halls of jests and cheers,
Multitudes here, with laughter, no fears.
Let's frolic through spaces, both odd and serene,
For in this grand joke, we're all on screen.

Rifts in Reality's Fabric

Dancing through rips in endless seams,
I trip on the fabric of stitched-up dreams.
My laundry's sent out on an intergalactic run,
While socks cheer for freedom, oh, what fun!

Bees in tuxedos play chess with mice,
Arguing fiercely about who's more nice.
Every corner turned reveals a new jest,
Where aliens host breakfast at the cosmos' behest.

Reality hiccups and spills its tea,
As the toaster demands it be set free.
With every rift, new antics arise,
Puns cavort and twirl before our eyes.

So let's embrace the quirks of our fate,
With giggles and gags, let's celebrate.
For in this wild tapestry, we'll forever play,
As the universe grins and says, "Stay!"

Dialogues Across Cosmic Fragments

In a realm where socks fly free,
Two cats debate eternity.
"Do you think we ever land?"
"Only if we shake a hand!"

A toaster toasted bread so bright,
It sparked a chat with a satellite.
"Why do you float?" it asked with glee,
"Because gravity's got no tea!"

A broomstick raced a comet fast,
"Catch me if you can, you blast!"
But the comet just laughed away,
"You sweep the floor, I make the day!"

A wormhole yawned, stretched out wide,
A raccoon leapt in, full of pride.
"What did I miss in this grand ride?"
"Just a couple of fries and a tide!"

Chronicles of Unseen Possibilities

In a world where cheese sings loud,
A mouse became an artist proud.
"I'll paint the sky with gouda cheer!"
"Just watch out for the flying deer!"

Outside a wormhole, a frog with flair,
Said, "I can leap beyond all care!"
But slipped on a bubble of time,
"Oop, missed my cue, my prime time!"

A rogue android made a cupcake,
"It's wired to impress, for goodness' sake!"
But when it danced, it broke a plate,
"Oh great, now I'm just second-rate!"

Two planets met for coffee beans,
Discussing life in cosmic scenes.
"Do you prefer a latte swirl?"
"I'll take it black, I'm not a whirl!"

Voices from Beyond the Veil

A ghost chuckled from an old book,
"You think I haunt? Just take a look!"
"I'm just here for the ghostly wit,"
"And maybe to steal a bit!"

An alien sipped starlight dew,
"Do you know why I'm here with you?"
"To borrow sugar, or so it seems,"
"And spread some intergalactic dreams!"

A talking chair claimed it felt wise,
"I've seen it all through human eyes!"
"Just keep the cushions nice and neat,"
"Or I'll throw you off and take a seat!"

A quantum cat played hide and seek,
With every turn, it'd disappear sneak.
"Where did it go? I swear I saw!"
"In another realm, it took a paw!"

Reflections in the Multiversal Mirror

Where reflections turn to silly sights,
A donut danced with joyful heights.
"I'm sweet enough to save the day!"
"Just watch your calories, I say!"

A speechless potato took a stand,
"I'm more than fries from the frying pan!"
It sprouted arms to lead a cheer,
"Viva la veggies, we've no fear!"

An old clock ticked with slower pace,
"Time doesn't rush, it takes its space.
But ask a rabbit, and you may hear,
"I run like crazy, never near!"

In a mirror, reflections shone bright,
"Any chance of turning day to night?"
"Just a twist of fate and a grin,
And let the cosmic fun begin!"

Dances of the Unfolding Narrative

In a universe where cats can talk,
They ponder life on a leisurely walk.
Dogs wear hats and sip their tea,
Debating if squirrels are truly free.

With every twist, a dance ensues,
Penguins dress up in bright, silly shoes.
Flap your arms, take a fresh spin,
Who knew a vacuum could hold such a win?

In one realm, toast flies through the air,
Butter landed beautifully with flair.
While waffles do their own wiggly jig,
Holding a party that's quite the big gig.

Thus laughter reigns in these cosmic plots,
Curiously weird, or just all hot shots?
Each tale woven, a giggle, a grin,
A tapestry bright where chaos begins.

Elysian Echoes of Possible Worlds

In a land where socks never match,
Fuzzy creatures plot their next catch.
Mice with capes zoom through the sky,
Chasing feathers that seem to fly high.

Meanwhile, fish are learning to dance,
In a river of milk, they take their chance.
With dolphins that boast their newest tricks,
Each splash of fun leaves everyone in a fix.

Clouds made of candy float on by,
As jellybeans rain from the marshmallow sky.
Unicorns giggle, chasing their tails,
While cupcakes sail on banana-peel gales.

What a sight to see this whimsy unfold,
In worlds where tales are entirely bold.
With laughter and joy, we twirl and spin,
Celebrating the fun that dwells deep within.

Threads of Cosmic Consciousness

An octopus wears a crown so bright,
Conducting the stars in cosmic delight.
Planets breakdance, round and round,
In this wild rhythm, they lose all sound.

Grapes wear glasses, reading the moon,
While broccoli hums a elevating tune.
Each veggie lively, they wiggle and sway,
With a rhythm that keeps dullness at bay.

Cacti don wigs as they stroll through the sand,
Debating the best flavor of jelly in hand.
With laughter echoing far into space,
Every moment is joined in a gleeful embrace.

In this splendid web of imagination,
Every idea bubbles with wild elation.
So let's fill our hearts with endless glee,
And dance with the cosmos 'neath the cosmic tree.

Songs of the Undergone

Beneath the surface, the critters cheer,
With secret bands playing tunes so clear.
Toadstools bouncing with rhythm and beat,
Boasting of jams that won't miss a seat.

A snail with dreams of rock star fame,
Practices hard to make his name.
While frogs croak ballads in cryptic prose,
And fireflies flash their disco clothes.

Worms in a conga line shimmy and slide,
Underneath dirt, they gather with pride.
Each note echoing a playful jest,
As an earthworm declares, 'This is the best!'

With laughter and music in every crack,
Lives the joy of the silly pack.
In the end, it's not just a song,
But a dance of life where we all belong.

Secrets of the Confluence

In a world where socks go missing,
I chased my cat through realms unblissing.
He claimed a throne of folded cloth,
While I just sighed, "Oh, what's the cloth?"

In parallel lives my coffee spills,
Each cup a laugh, each sip a thrill.
Baristas wink from worlds afar,
As I spill dreams beneath a star.

Wormholes weave through laundromat lanes,
Where time's a jester playing games.
My laundry dances, laughs in the breeze,
While I'm caught up in cosmic tease.

Snap! A universe jumps the queue,
I'm startled awake, in a blink I'm blue.
But hey, I think I'll take a ride,
With mismatched socks as my guide!

Narratives of Cosmic Drift

In a realm of mismatched twins,
One plays chess, the other spins.
They argue over who's the best,
While I just laugh and take my rest.

Galactic gossip travels wide,
A comet's tale from far and wide.
Aliens snicker at our plight,
As I inquire, "Is that a flight?"

In dance of stars, I see a joke,
Planets twirl beneath the cloak.
I step on shadows, trip on light,
As gravity gives me quite the fright.

Slipping through dimensions, I grin,
Riding waves of cosmic spin.
Each twist, a riddle wrapped in cheer,
As laughter echoes, drawing near!

Serpents of Time and Space

A serpent slithers through the clock,
Ticking softly, mocking luck.
I pet its head, it laughs with glee,
"Have you got time for tea with me?"

Dimensions fold like old cheese pie,
As I ponder, "Oh, why not try?"
I'm chased by time with silly twists,
And find it's all just a mad bliss.

Once I met a wise old sage,
Who flipped through time like a comic page.
He grinned and said, "You'll always frown,
Unless you wear that silly crown!"

So I donned it, laughed, spun in place,
With serpents twirling, holding space.
In this dance, I found my grace,
While time and laughter interlace!

Portraits of the Unexplored

In galleries of worlds unseen,
I wandered through with a curious keen.
Each portrait grinned, eyes wide with jest,
As they whispered, "Welcome to the quest!"

One depicted a cat in a hat,
Reciting rhymes, how about that?
While beside it lay a dog so wise,
With glasses on, it rolled its eyes.

Beneath each canvas laughed a plot,
Of space-time shenanigans, a tangled knot.
They winked and danced, a merry crew,
Inviting me to join their view.

So I took a seat, enjoyed the show,
Where laughter bubbled, and chaos flowed.
At the end of the day, I felt so sure,
That portraits hold secrets, laughter pure!

Scribbles from the Void

In a corner of nowhere, I scribble with glee,
My pen flips through portals, oh what do I see?
Cats wear top hats, dancing on clouds,
While fish ride bicycles, laughing out loud.

Jellybeans rain from a bright orange sun,
As robots play chess, just for fun.
Pigs in pajamas float by on a breeze,
I pause for a moment, and think, "Oh, please!"

The coffee flows freely from a tall tree,
But the cups are too small; they just giggle at me.
A frog runs for office, promising flies,
While unicorns jump to reach blueberry pies.

In this space where chaos routinely collides,
Unbelievable nonsense just never hides.
So I'll scribble some more on my whimsical page,
Creating a circus of humor and sage.

Starlit Dialogues of Dreamscapes

Under starlit skies, the dreams come alive,
To chat with a cupcake, I'd pay quite a drive.
"It's sweet in here!" shouts a blueberry whale,
While a rabbit in glasses recounts his old tale.

Clouds dressed in pajamas float over the moon,
As spoons have a meeting to discuss how to swoon.
A knight in a tutu goes searching for gold,
But finds only socks and a mystery bold.

"Why do we dream?" asks a wise old chair,
"I think we're just bored!" says a cat with a stare.
The penguins in bowties agree with a cheer,
"We'll keep up the chatter without any fear!"

So when night draws near, and worlds shift and sway,
Remember the dialogues we have in play.
With laughter at dawn and a sigh at the dusk,
These starlit exchanges turn dreams into husk.

Chronicles of the Conditional

If wishes had wheels, I'd roll through the sky,
With a squirrel in a cape flying effortlessly high.
I'd barter my troubles for glitter and giggles,
While time-traveling turtles make spontaneous wiggles.

What if bread could sing, would toasters rejoice?
If socks found their partners, would they have a voice?
Whimsical thoughts dance in knots around my head,
As dreams sprout wings and soar out of bed.

Perhaps lions would purr like kittens in disguise,
While stars knit the universe with colorful ties.
Imagine a world where monotony's banned,
And every dull moment gets flipped on the hand.

In these chronicles penned with a wink and a smile,
Life's little absurdities stretch on for a mile.
So ponder the what-ifs that tickle your brain,
For whimsical chaos is always insane.

Tales from the Other Side of Reality

On the other side where oddities roam,
A taco teaches salsa as it searches for home.
This world's upside down, where odd laws persist,
And time often slips away like a wisp.

Mirrors hold meetings, debating their style,
While fish on scooters swim with a smile.
A lion with a job runs a bakery stall,
Serving pastries to foxes, they're having a ball!

The grass is all purple, the sun sings reggae,
Napping on clouds is the ultimate way.
If you visit my kingdom, don't forget to bring,
A spoon for the laughter, let joy take wing!

So gather your friends from all realms and plans,
For tales full of whimsy stretch long like a span.
In this curious land, where nonsense is real,
Every chuckle and giggle becomes part of the deal.

The Dance of Diverging Worlds

In one world, cats wear hats,
While dogs play chess in spats.
A goldfish swims in a tiny car,
As cows write books and strum on guitar.

In another place, trees chat with bees,
And squirrels run races while drinking teas.
The clouds do the cha-cha in the sky,
While rainbows sip coffee and ask 'Oh my?'

Somewhere else, kings wear pajamas,
While queens bake cakes of sweet iguanas.
A hamster dreams of being a knight,
Wielding a sword, ready to fight!

So let's travel where laughter reigns,
In realms of joy, without the pains.
Each twist and turn, just a fun surprise,
In these world dances, who knows what lies?

Chronicles of the Infinite Divide

In a dimension where socks all walk,
And teapots gossip, oh how they talk!
The sun wears sunglasses at noon,
While clocks tick-tock to a funky tune.

There's a land where gravity's just a joke,
And starfish tell knock-knock jokes to folk.
The hills are steep, made of mashed potatoes,
Where every cat and dog is a top-rated potato.

In the next corner, cupcakes fly,
And toast with butter aims for the sky.
A snail can time travel—slowly, of course,
While reindeer navigate with potato force.

Each version of life, a quirky spin,
Where nothing's lost and laughter begins.
So grab a slice of this comic plight,
And dance with me through the stars tonight!

Symbols of Sunsets and Supernovas

Across the glow of flaming skies,
Pineapples wear glasses, oh what a surprise!
Dancing with stars that wink and twinkle,
While comets share secrets with a sprinkle.

In one sunbeam, a crab plays chess,
With a fish who claims it's nobody's mess.
A moon made of cheese grins with delight,
As galaxies giggle, holding on tight.

There, crayons draw portraits of silly clouds,
Each one wearing hats that are rather loud.
A parrot recites poems to the wind,
As skies nod in rhythm, their laughter pinned.

So toast to the sunsets, the wonders they bring,
In a world that's as wacky as a circus ring.
With your quirky companions, let's fly high,
Through symbols of laughter as stars pass by!

Interludes of All That Could Be

In an interlude where bananas sing,
And cupcakes dance with a dash of bling.
Where pizza delivers, wearing a tie,
And owls explore dreams that fly high.

There's a universe where frogs wear shoes,
And caterpillars spin webs of good news.
A cosmic colander filters out the frowns,
While jellybeans bob through candy towns.

In a realm of playlists made of ice cream,
With rhythms so sweet, they make you beam.
The rain tickles flowers, they laugh in delight,
As fairy lights twinkle throughout the night.

So let's enjoy these interludes bold,
Crafting stories with colors untold.
In the world of imagination, we are the key,
Unlocking the joy of all that could be!

Dreams Entwined in Multifarious Paths

In one world, I'm a cat on a mat,
Chasing dust motes like a diplomat.
In another, I bake cakes made of cheese,
Where everyone dances with sprightly ease.

In yet another, I'm a knight with no quest,
Just hanging out with a duck in a vest.
We're plotting to rule with a pie and a grin,
While the cookies look on, thinking, "Where do we fit in?"

Across a dimension, I juggle some glue,
Which sticks to my nose like some crazy new hue.
And the fish in the sky make a splashy ballet,
While I look up and think, "What a weird kind of day!"

So here's to the realms where chaos reigns,
Where my duplicates prance with silly refrains.
If you trip through the vortex, don't take it to heart,
Just laugh at your life—a truly grand art!

Intersections of Unrealized Futures

At the corner of dreams and absurd designs,
I met my clone, who sells whimsy in lines.
He offered me socks made of broccoli heads,
While aliens pondered on chocolate baguettes.

In a timeline where Mondays are always fun,
The workweek is just a bizarre little pun.
With unicorns teaching us stand-up routine,
And laughter erupts like a shimmering scene.

I peeked at a future where toasters take flight,
And buttered toast sings a tune, pure delight.
We navigate bubbles, all squeaky and bright,
With mismatched socks as our fashion insight.

So let's raise a toast to unrealized fate,
As we bounce through dimensions and munch on a crate.
With a giggle or two as our guiding star,
Who knew that being weird was the best way to go far?

Whispers Over the Divide

From the edge of my porch to the stars up high,
I heard whispers of cats, who claim they can fly.
A riddle in shadows, a dance of delight,
While squirrels debate what's more comfy at night.

On Monday, I'm dreaming of pirates and loot,
While Tuesday's a garden with talking radish roots.
And Wednesday's for frogs, who wear silly hats,
Arguing fiercely—"Who's the best at doing spats?"

With a beam of bright laughter drifting across space,
I found my reflection in an upside-down face.
It winked and it grinned, with its paws in the air,
And said, "Life's just a dance—a wild, joyous affair!"

So here's to the echoes that tease and collide,
With whispers of nonsense on a thrilling ride.
Let's leap through the cracks in our quirky design,
And embrace all the fun of this wild pantomime!

Colors of the Celestial Spectrum

In a realm where the sun wears a fuchsia tie,
And rainbows are made of a green apple pie.
The stars like to hum, while the comets play tag,
As the universe giggles—a vibrant old hag.

Each hue tells a story, all jumbled and spry,
With violet wishes that shimmer and sigh.
A pink cookie planet spins sweetly around,
While laughter erupts from the starry ground.

Oh, how the oranges dance with the blues,
In a swirling performance, they've nothing to lose.
With splashes of laughter in gauzy delight,
The cosmos performs on a stage made of light.

So let's paint our dreams in the wildest of tones,
Making music with colors, as lively as phones.
In this spectrum of chaos, let's roll up our sleeves,
And create our own worlds, with joy that never leaves!

www.ingramcontent.com/pod-product-compliance
Lightning Source LLC
Chambersburg PA
CBHW051641160426
43209CB00004B/737